KINDER PARASITES

Holly Moberley (she/they) is a queer poet and poison berry from the South East. She is a Poetry Society Young Critic and has been published in *fourteen poems*, *Bi+Lines*, *Butcher's Dog,* & *The North*. She is Bristol's 2021 LYRA Slam Champion and is currently touring a spoken word show on CPR and the drowning girl motif.

PRAISE for *Kinder Parasites:*

Moberley's writing is delicious, oozing with pleasure at every step. These are tender, enticing poems - instructions on how to live.

— Chloe Elliott

These exclamatory poems parse the queer panic of your 20s with urgency and wit. 'Welcome to not-girl summer,' writes Moberley, 'make yourself at home.'

— Helen Bowell

Kinder Parasites is a brilliant and buzzing debut. Moberley catapults from Katy Perry in space to Caroline Calloway in a therapist's office, the glittering beacons of girlboss feminism becoming spectres in a collection that balances humour and pathos as it splits apart any expectation of what's coming next. *Kinder Parasites* simmers with irreverence as Moberley teases us through the disappointments and elations of being a person in the world; it is endlessly fun and always surprising.

— Ciara Maguire

Explosive in its refusal to conform, bold in its language and beautiful in its embrace of the grotesque. There's an exhilarating rebelliousness in how this clear-eyed debut pamphlet whiplashes us from pop and internet culture to literary reference to body horror and back. This is an unapologetic joy ride of poems by Holly Moberley. In *Kinder Parasites*, exclamation marks become totems, pages become playgrounds for structural invention, and poetry is a vessel that excavates what it means to be a queer woman making sense of herself in a world pulling her in every direction. Every page turn holds a surprise. Once read, these poems will live in your body forever.

— Malaika Kegode

ISBN: 978-1-917617-39-0

Cover designed by Aaron Kent

Edited and Typeset by Aaron Kent

Broken Sleep Books Ltd
PO BOX 102
Llandysul
SA44 9BG

CONTENTS

Kinder Parasites

Holly Moberley

Broken Sleep Books

Oh this feeling has drenched my bones, and turned my skeleton pink.
— Hera Lindsay Bird

Bear, I love you. Pull my head off.
— Marian Engel

ALL THIS TALK OF GOTHIC LOVE IS MAKING ME WANT TO BURST INTO FLAMES…

for Megan Fox, sans Machine Gun Kelly

how dare you need to live forever !

how dare you choose eternity !

shrivel up and garden like the rest of us

quit spilling your expensive blood, we get it

you have the interviews, you glitter in the sun !!

your juicy body is incapable of dehydration

it makes us sick !!

this is the fantasy of cannibalism

butchered by armie hammer

this is the fantasy of armie hammer

butchered by cannibalism

this tool for impacts swung in reverse

an affair where you cheat on yourself

O megan ! we know you're out there ! come home !

your heart is a hummingbird frisbeed into a gramophone

your pulse is so sombre shostakovich won't hear it

i know you want instructions on how to live

you worry about breaking before the crockery

i'm sending you a curse where you can only say sorry

one that makes you love yourself more

11

BAMBIFICATION

like a chaise lounge, like wet silk.   His musket

a parting in the woods

the thicket,   some good milk,

Now, the wolves tie up your clothing as if you are departed.

*

When you cry with the day, a berry bush unfruits!

When you cry with the night, you undo the forest.

*

My mother, you sold me:

...

called him an artist

it sold me: the shambles, some poor hunger,

Every time he guillotines your sculpture,

I imagine two more (mothers) will sprout in your place.

*

Somewhere nearby, a temple crumbles.

nowhere to hide to

unshuck the daughter.

13

Just last week we met a man

who stole cuttings from   Monet's garden and v

I'M SO BORED I THINK I'LL START A CULT I'M SO BORED I THINK I'LL RUIN YOUR LIFE

A group of bats is 'a cauldron'. A group of cobras; 'a quiver.' Lemurs; 'a conspiracy' like they pointed their striped tails subliminally and decided hayfever is a theory. The truth is an ultrasound, only some animals can hear it. The rest of us are busy wiping our pheromones on good trees and hoping they'll stick. So what if I've been abandoned ?? So what if I'm too coarse to be a ghost ?? It's hard to stay elusive when all you want to do is roll down the Hollywood Hills in Jodie Comer's pink dress. All you want to do is play the enchanted flute, leading straight children astray like the queer pied piper. *My name is Kinder Parasite, nice to meet you.* She who will offer them everything. She who will lead them down the dark dark forest of fan pages for hands and lesbians in the US cabinet. Here ye !! Here ye !! *Woman in the market for some atrocious sunsets.* Gotta hold someone responsible, these skies are that intimate. Oh, my evenings are so lonely I gave a CPR dummy the power of breath. Now she won't stop ending our conversations with a sigh.

UNIVERSAL TORTURE DEVICE TORTURES ME PERSONALLY

What is a word but the vehicle we drive back & forth?
  – Ella Frears[1]

like a trapdoor in a castle leading to a dungeon full of... concepts
like a sinister toaster that only cares about revenge...

forcing the confession of my lackluster crimeography... silence
in the manor court... never once pleasing the scribe... regretting
always using my indoor voice, even when i used to go outside

lighting up the candles on my personal punishment cake... flavour
everlasting !! my torment... so deliciously specific and niche... so
unlike any other soreness

officiating my marriage to the love of my life whose suit is sewn
with black-legged ticks... where i kiss her on the lips that are
red-legged ticks... struggle to put the ring on her ring finger which
is a crawling mess of pacific coast ticks... wondering how i loved her
for so long without noticing this... her short life cycles... the
constant need she had to get under my skin

pain... that ghost train full of no-one riding off a cliff... that
groundbreaking eureka that no-one has ever and will henceforth
feel as bad as this.... one-hundred black cats at the black cat
audition... baring one-hundred hairballs of grief...

---

1. See 'Sestina for Caroline Bergvall', Ella Frears.

agony   my fuzzy ochre torment that keeps on returning

poetry   my wet pink grotto granting hungry mouths a wish

writing is my grief tourism… it's renting out the monument… when locals visit for free… it's my emotional sightseeing, my most ritzy route to torture, my expecting release

DESIRE FOR A FUTURE PORCH ON WHICH TO PLAY MY FUTURE BANJO

i've rarely held paradise but this will do fine; lacy insects

impractical to the touch

and me, stepping through the mosquito net, looking at our rental

dead in the eyes

which are your eyes by association… *amphibious green…*

the whole palo verde…

and what did we expect ?? this is what happens when an architect

and a landscape gardener

have sex for the first time; they climax in fleshy succulents,

sticky hibiscus pinks,

an entire rustic porch !! ++ plus banjo ++ plus stool

architectural digest = desperate to broaden their audience.

no this is not the poem

in which i imagine my air bnb host is starring in an

interior design porno

but the garden is a setup. the setup is a sexy fire blazing

all over the hills…

fuck whoever in the land of the free !! too much sun

on the mountainside[2]

---

2. See *The Uneven Distribution of AI's Environmental Impacts* on Harvard Business Review by Shaolei Ren and Adam Wierman.

but fuck whoever !! if you fire your arrows into clay pots

they'll photosynthesize and become the whole

homophobic tree for achilles' ghost to hate.

the birds were windchimes in another life — the windchimes

were running water

with the hollywood glitz left in. can you tell i am trying not

to be jaded

as i imagine the future? can you tell it's the same light on my

fingers so gold it peeled paint after paint

from off the front porch?

REVENGE THEORY
after kandace siobhan walker [3]

i want to open a factory where we repurpose skateboards into nail files for horses / do you give out permits for this kind of thing / i need to know i have your support / the town planner says so you want to build an eyesore in the centre of town / i say how about a mill / they're a lot more quaint in their destruction / i'll need some stables and a paddock too / she says why don't you sneak vegetables into his plasterboard and be done with it / the town planner is gnawing her pencil down to the wick / i ask don't you get bored sometimes / yes / isn't it better to be in love and bored of someone else / yes / than out of love and skate-bored of yourself / she says she's not qualified enough to answer the question / she says this city's not built for fresians / but think of the influx of horses / their happy hooves / think of my ex's face when every skateboard he's ever owned gradually goes missing / she says i think you need to let it go / i say can't you see i am / i'm finding new hobbies / i'm fogging up my ex's windows with mill smoke eternally / my equestrian shaped smog ruining the view / the town planner says there is such a thing as going too far / i say where is it / take me to the point on a map / i'll ride there with my herd of grateful city horses / it'll be like the first man on the moon / i'll drive my bitter flag into the ground knowing no-one has taken it this far before / i will kidnap as many skateboards as required / i will file as many hooves as there are horses / i need a four legged epitome warm on my thighs / i need a place for love to live / to look at this gift city in the mouth and trust that it still belongs to me

3. See delightful 'Astronaut' by Kandance Siobhan Walker

SPEED DATING BUT I SAT DOWN OPPOSITE A GRAVE DIGGER; WHEN ASKED ABOUT HER PROFESSION THIS IS WHAT SHE SAID:

My problem is, always, what to confess,
  — Ella Frears[4]

when the dead body tried to write about love it lost another arm...

no when the dead body tried to write about love it pissed all over

the floor !! that was a rumi[5] poem... but i've been wrong before

btw i'm just business casual khakis and the gates i've pried open

what are coffins but surfboards to the afterlife? fun ways

to accessorise when the general advice is to remain sombre and swim

my mother says when the time comes could i spray her over a cliff

her urn hissing like an aerosol... full of ashes... full of nonstop dead

mother...

this is badness: a mafioso sizing up a crypt

it's like buying a local mansion that you won't let anyone live in

and then moving to spain... leaving behind everyone who remains

alive in a bread crumb trail of dereliction

4. See 'Barbara Writes to the Reverend', Ella Frears.

5. See Rumi ".. *a pen went scribbling along. When it tried to write love, it broke.*"

like saying; *i bought us a jacuzzi but you have to sit this one out*
leave me alone to soak in my luxury death… with bubbles…
with underwater heating… all the while slipping down the
multipurpose lift to hell… where the denim speedos stay on

i paint on each private mausoleum with the sharpest saddest stick:
HERE LIES THE TOWN'S WORST WASTE
OF REALLY NICE ACOUSTICS

how completely unnecessary !!! lay down in the bog !!!
don't be a baby… i've had it with your hors d'oeuvres at the wake
& your gated communities… your winking anime eggs looking at me…
like a pair of ovaries… your rude potential of life… like a glitter-cry of…
nepo baby

even the dead deserve a holiday… even the dead don't stay buried…
my favourite books talk about exhuming like it's easy !!
there are the songs i listen to on repeat: this one goes
la la la i'd carry a shovel wherever i went if they weren't so heavy[6]

people think i don't believe in anything but my faith walks differently;
is a shadow that only comes out during specific times of day
the stars deadding up the night… with their long distance dead light

6. To be sung to the tune of Kylie Minogue's 'Can't Get You Out of My
Head'.

21

all around me nice remains will sequin out of existence like virtual

leaves from a gone-bad kingdom… on bad days i shake my owls

from trees for the whooshing noise that comes with them

welcome to not-girl summer, make yourself at home !!

i'm always undoing what has already been done

what remains of me is scared of making a too harsh mark

on the world… of loving what i love too badly…

these weird years i've wasted, being usefully vacant

swinging my duffel into the next supernatural event

HOUDINI'S RABBIT ON HER TIME IN THE HAT

It's important to note that for a time spiritualism was one of the only ways women were allowed to speak in public.
— Danielle La Rock[7]

YOU WANT TO KNOW HOW HE DID IT / ALL THESE YEARS / AND THE QUESTIONS ARE STILL THE SAME / I'M BIG FOR A RABBIT BUT ALL THESE MEN ARE BIGGER / IT'S WHY WOMEN ARE ASSISTANTS AND NEVER MAGICIANS / DON'T THEY HAVE SUCH SMALL HANDS / IF YOU WORK 'EM TOO HARD WON'T THEY SHRIVEL / LIKE BEACHED STARFISH / GASPING / BEFORE HOUDINI / I SAW COUNTLESS MEN THROW DAGGERS THROUGH WOMEN / STRAPPED TO A SPINNING CIRCUS WHEEL ON CONEY ISLAND / THE CROWDS WENT WILD / DROPPING CANDY FLOSS AND CHIRPING "GOOD SHOW" "OLD SPORT" "GOOD SHOW" / LIKE A ROOM FULL 'O HUNGRY BIRDS / WHAT WOULDN'T I HAVE DONE FOR A SHRED OF LETTUCE BACK THEN / I LET THE GIRLS SPIN ON LIKE ROTISSERIE / THEIR EYES WIDE SHUT / TRACING OUT PRAYERS / ASKING FOR FORGIVENESS FROM SOME FATAL DEFICIENCY / LIKE ME / THEY WERE TAUGHT TO CURL IN ON THEMSELVES IN THE DARK

---

7. National Park After Dark Podcast, 182: A Good Ol' Fashioned Séance. Presidents Park. Interesting to consider that the American séance was one of the first instances in which women were able to speak in public.

WHILE THE REST OF US GET HISTORY, QUEER GIRLS GET FABLES
for Alice Brown and Emma Ainsworth [8]

get two women   !!!   get feet !!!   sweet fruit and wine !!!

get living together for fifty years and refusing to marry
their autumns hot to the touch and blistering on knowing that

never again is the miasma of trees so warm and unspooling
get historians who tell you   they were Best Friends
they lived alone in a one bed house   as Best Friends do !!!

kept warm under the same linen   looking a lot like Best Friends
scholars conjure them squealing over boys !!!
unravelling in their nightgowns   a pillow's width apart

sipping each other's breath into old age like Aesop's parched foxes
i mean Best Friends   this is the nineteenth century !!!
queer people haven't been invented yet

and it's always pitch dark past noon !!!
we're all just sat here waiting on Thomas Edison
if Alice and Emma held hands
know that it was under the cover of night

---

8. See the fictional Reductress article *Historians Pretty Sure Two Women Who Lived and Were Buried Together Just Friends.*

they had their eyes closed   like Best Friends would !!!

when spitting out the names of men and drowning in the dewy moon

Alice   guiding Emma to the fig tin   considering each finger

knowing how the licked open insides   in no time   begin to stick

AFTER LOSING ALL HOPE, I EMBRACE THE FURDOM
Draw your pleasure, paint your pleasure and express your pleasure strongly.
— Pierre Bonnard

i could tell you with my sphynx, i could tell you with my

similarly spelt word that tenses at an opening...

being an artist is a totally un-mortifying experience

you pray someone will pluck you from a line of thirty eight equally

eligible cats, thirty eight equally eligible catchelors... dragging their

cartoon x's over the carpets in unison...

someone who likes me for the excessive muscles in my ears !

someone who likes me for my post-litterbox confidence !

the ultraviolet in my eye

my yarn to chase and chase as it unfurls at the slightest touch takes

the form of approval... reveals its own end... meow, this cosmic joke !!

this spiders leg i eventually made crawl !!

this desperate wanting to be more than a seasonal spectacle

someplace close, success takes shape on the premise of a

completely unbroken window

to gain entrance, i'd groom my fur and empty it of how to

maintain a flat fringe in the wind

to gain entrance, i'd lick my privates in record speed; unsticking
all my best kept and culturally valuable secrets

my fur-mate coughs up balls of wise and
wild nuggets, returns blackbirds to the nest
me, i hunt the whole street. i hunt the whole woods and pets at homes
everywhere; hissy and romancaphobic, a vantablack bath mat slung
over a bush of roses

pierre bonnard used to sneak into galleries and touch up his paintings,
misleading security — pierre in fake whiskers dabbing milk pigment
over le chat blanc[9] like france's most passionate furry:

"that's not pierre it's the whitest french cat !!! he confuses the eye !!!"

we are all afraid of being found out... accused of some creative
deceit... what's scarier than being called a genius is knowing what that
means and then having to hold onto it for dear life

pierre bonnard avec night terrors... pierre bonnard during stress
induced sleep... thrown from the highest window of the fur-court,
after failing to please the fur-queen... his stash of mon dieu's flying
out behind him

---

9. See pedaliza's r/museum post for public opinion on 'Pierre Bonnard —
The White Cat (1894)'

his mind gone white recalling all the cats he's ever loved and
tried to be... the eight legged brawls and freshly uncapped milk...
hoards of defeatable mice... catnip binges with maurice

the most picturesque parts of feline living... each one surfacing
then slipping from him like fleas...

and maybe true meaning is the cats we played along the way and
maybe pierre's nine lives are still stretching out before him even now...
picking up nine separate scents

"it was never the paintings of the cats it was the cats held up inside
them !!" pierre meows, somehow still falling "yowl ! mrrrrrr !" cries
pierre, as the impossibly placed quagmire rises up to meet him...
for once he doesn't try to catch the likeness

LAST REMAINING SUBSCRIBER
after Caroline Calloway and her literary onlyfans

sarasota orchid

stepping off a plane

this entire uber drive

no-one in the lobby

the theme of her thumbnail

a fiery car crash[10]

fume-finessed

daisy buchanan

topless and framed

by flowers juliet

capulet bewildered

and behind on her

laundry talking for

a year about matisse

in her grey garden

gatsby what gatsby

shifty sage by the

ancestral portrait

grandmother who

grandmother who

gave the fixtures

---

10. See Lily Anolik's Vanity Fair piece — Caroline Calloway Survived
Cancellation. Now She's Doubling Down.

their useless anatomy

outdated the armoire

it girl rides throbbing

fiasco finishes with

a lemon wedge

for there never was a sour

vulva sour this sweet

crouching down better

inside the garden   ingénue

WEST COAST MULTIPLE CHOICE

Space is going to finally be glam. Let me tell you something. We are going to put the 'ass' in astronaut.
— Katy Perry[11]

all through saving they had tried to warn me off you, said los angeles is as much a place to stay in as katy perry albums are bespoke hotels for dogs[12]. ever since stepping off the plane i've waited to arrive, but all around me are better departures; people slipping in from the dry and restless air. angelenos packing multiple toothbrushes then going someplace else. one minute i was catching an uber from LAX, the next i was wide eyed with technical optimism — pointing out googie restaurants (which is the drag of american architecture); those fast food diners that could serve you a burger and then fly you off to space[13]. along the freeway i make a poem from the arrival of billboards: *asteroid city... red western rock... our feminist urge to vanquish the sky...* holy toledo! there goes a man selling tasers by the metro, there goes every possible avenue with the _____

a.) dimmest of stars

b.) bleakest of palms

c.) whitest of bars

11. See Vrinda Jagota's article for Pitchfork: 'In Space, No One Can Hear You Girlboss'.

12. Inspired by Alice Cappelle's video essay *liberal feminism is dying — now what?*

13. See Gill Scott Heron's poem 'Whitey on the Moon'.

SOMEONE GAVE CAROLINE CALLOWAY THE SWIVEL CHAIR AND NOW SHE WON'T STOP THINKING SHE'S A THERAPIST

don't be shy   hands up, acolytes come clean,

anyone who   is regularly disturbed

by their own   crepuscular activity,

everyone who is   anyone who has no-one

to cover their   head in cake,

spines realign   all over my clinic

chairs turn around   all over my office

to the sound of a   hundred dollar franklin

swimming his way   out from your pocket,

massive influence   lives in the water

and it is your duty   to drink a glass of both,

moisturise, elbows up,   remember to breathe,

javelin your pristine sadness   into the nearest baddest sea

whenever i cry, the whole of   arizona gets down on its knees,

our sorrow is so smart   our sorrow will always decorate a home

while we are a pillow   in a burrow and so mad

we're not the whole   soft bedroom,

permission, take my   glittering permission,

live like teleshopping   would've wanted

where the only words   you can say are

BRIGHT   BRILLIANT   BAGS

theatrical and fondling   the zips,

two gay dolphins croaking
i knew a girl once in sarasota,
right, she patiently spoke in
till she was crushed by
forgive me, the moss here
the moss here is leftover
hush, lay down now, lay down
we can envy the cabana boy

the marina, the marina,
she did every single thing
timid wet reptiles
the mouth of an ancient diagnosis
the moss is coincidental
from a yoga residential,
in the hectic green
for how women on sunbeds
call his name

#38TH REASON TO LIVE IN THE CAVE

this city is so loud   its supermarkets   so unlike a clearing in the woods

how is anyone   supposed to frolic   in this lighting

how is anyone   supposed to flirt well   in this economy

where the most i   have in common   with anybody is

the perishables   the urgency   with which we eat

i could be a fruit bat   with its echolocation   set to catastrophe

my tendency towards   avoidance making the   doom prophecy come true i'm a chiroptera!   get me out of here   do what you have to do

out of hell!   out of evil young legs!   out of the deeply personal moon!

my wings which   once unfolded like   a leaflet spreads open

are now each a   glinting axe for   cutting trees to ruin[14]

---

14. Moberley gets its origins from the name Mobberly in Cheshire.
The place name derives from Old English mōt 'meeting' + burg 'fortress' + lēah 'woodland clearing'.

35

EVERY HISTORICAL EVENT GETS SUCKED INTO A SINKHOLE ON VALENTINES DAY AND NOW THE WHOLE OF HISTORY IS HAPPENING AT ONCE

it's cuffing   season!! i will

be tying myself to the   nearest tree and refusing

to see reason. toss your coins into my open mouth & i will

swallow you a wish like if a blowjob had magical powers. the

story of cinderella is that you can flee the scene & a man in

epaulettes will delight in your absence. patriarchal romance!

this woman lived it — every shade of cave: ovens, glass

slippers, no-privacy caskets, one deep breath locked

in ice beside a mammoth. riddle me this — my

own two feet in the cold, the glacial aunt

of bermuda seas & crime novel

mist. once i entered

the shoe shop

and

asked if they had   any incels. once i

asked for sandals & left   with a scandal on each of

my feet. hold a gladius[15] to my head & i will go off on one

like the one roman soldier everybody hates. tiberius is nice

but he won't stop talking about capitalism & critiquing the

saints!!! it's spoiling the dinner! it's ruining bathtime for

all of us! i will be in the heat of battle telling the

other side we invented nomenclators [16] &

communal ass sponges in the same

breath. i could tell you i've

loved before

but

37

---

15. 'Gladius' (Latin): a particular sword used by Roman soldiers.
16. 'Nomenclatures' (Latin) were employed by Roman aristocrats, whose responsibilities included recalling the names of people their master met during political campaigns.

that's like saying   i've done the
washing when instead i   threw my pants at a mitski
concert. i've barely broken the yeast-smelling surface. everything
you've heard about me is true!!! it's always unattractive crying &
never Elton John's Immortalised Tears. love is an old lady with a
'water me sign' speaking in tongues. 19th century hysteria sans
beach!! sans the relief of clutching my shawl!! love is missing
someone so much you plant their eyelashes in soil, sew
their scabs into a tasteful, modest toga. 999,
        what's your emergency? love
                has flown
                    here

like a gargoyle   from the 13th

century. with wings   on!! like the worst kind

of post!! like something you wouldn't want to fall on

your head. advice on the phone is stay low, don't move

love is starting a horse themed war for you, is acting

goofy around planks of wood, ultimately isolating

the Helens, again! i could be making waves at

the symposium[17] or learning how to look

good but whittle better & i'm

stuck here thinking up

ways to be

clever

39

---

17. 'Symposium' (Latin): referring to a convival party (often after a banquet) featuring an exchange of ideas and or a discussion of significant matters.

WHAT TO DO WHEN NICOLE KIDMAN DOESN'T LOVE YOU

a hair dying montage, hotels with swimming pools, inflatable

flamingos, valuing my REM cycle,

scientology, pawning heterosexual jewellery,

boldly declining to experience a crush, crushing, being

crushed, telling my crush about said crush

in question, resisting the urge to walk into a lamppost

while awaiting her voice note. her voice like

nothing i've ever noted   before.

i heard   that the red lights of amsterdam were first

lit in the district of her mouth.

i heard   she was limping home in the after hours

of an old european city like some mystical wolf.

how 12th century gothic, how unintentionally

twilight.

crush; she makes me want to listen to mazzy star,

she makes me want to mope around the house

in an unwashed dressing gown.

in this light, i am like if a lava lamp was a girl. i am

       the gooey colour of gay panic.

to get there you have to take a left at clara's gym

       shorts and exit onto serena's surfer girl

shoulders.

the difference between me and regency era dramas

       is that i hide my ability to evangelise.

i have been known to cry into a fortune telling mirror.

       i have been known to call this self care.

when you're a queer woman, anything you do

       becomes provocative.

you could be reclaiming rhinestones into your

       wardrobe and all of a sudden it's

because your crush is busy speaking to someone else.

i keep asking but my metaphors won't swallow me

       whole. they say "no amount of pop-culture

references can save you now"

but i'm a femme tom cruise on bad filler benders

       and she's so nicole-kidman-post-divorce,

it hurts.

TERRA INCOGNITA [18]

with you — there are bright pink rabbits for punctuation

the latin dying inside me feels useful

we spend time putting woodpeckers back on their rightful branches

i comb for words like *capsicum* and *opuntia*

desperate to catch up — with my all-fours-of-language

to move you solely with sounds ! hark ! *how hard she fetches breath* [19]

only the prairie dog[20] digs fast enough

only rodents speak well with soil in their teeth

---

18. *Terra Incognita* (meaning "unknown land" in Latin) was a term used by cartographers for regions that had not yet been mapped or explored.

19. From Shakespeare's play Henry IV: "Hark, how hard he fetches breath."

20. See *The Surprising Complexity of Prairie Dog Language* article for Atlas Obscura.

ALL MY FRIENDS ARE WORM CHARMING

they are out there ... touching england's green grass without me
        sucking up the cornish vistas to themselves !! like a mix
between augustus gloop and bob ross
        in the surrounding meadows even the thrushes are greedy
for more colour than usual
        & forever some news anchor is being cruel about the sport...

i should've been a contender with her cowboy hat that cooes
             SEXY INVERTEBRATES !!!
        in a slowed down barry manilow voice at various
inappropriately timed intervals

i would've worn a latex crow mask to tap on their worm homes
        like the coming rain
mirroring deceitfully our cycle of life !! they'd never see me
        coming... which has nothing to do with
having no eyes & everything to do with my dynamic ingenuity

i could've come on to the older men in their pink high vis jackets
        answering to WORM JUDGE
i'm gay ... but i could've been straight for thirty minutes... for the
        extra points & the revolving worm trophy...i would've
done that for the good of the team

ours is a kind of friendship symbiosis, you're like the iconic &

    nationally loved bumble… i'm like

the flower that dies if it doesn't get any attention

all my dearest are at the feet-out hangout

    & i have FOWO !!²¹ charged with the ethical erotica

of caring too much… first it's not wanted for worm charming,

    next for housewarmings then birthdays and funerals

one day

    the world will yawn into extinction & the only thing

we'll have in common is how much we miss milk

    oblivious to our respective profundity & stuck in a mutual

yearn for artisanal cheeses !!! global warming… the goats get smaller

    everyday²²… you never call

what do you mean *we were just like minded individuals* ???

    our friendship was supposed to transcend the boundaries

---

21. ACRONYM meaning Fear of Worming Out. Derived from FOMO meaning Fear of Missing Out. EXAMPLE: When you want to go to the party but you don't think you're worm-enough. "Stacy's not coming. She's scared of worming out."

22. See Tom Mason's research essay on the chamois 'Environmental Change and long-term body mass.'

of reason & screen time

       our friendship was supposed to be made into a feature length;
the cast of alien (1979) starring as our worm-selves

+ millipedes who moonlight as combs, pull out knots in the grass,
       returning confidence by the strand
where we are close in the way that all eyeless creatures in the
       ground are close... the comradery of knowing that
not everyone can learn to live like this;
       our language, our customs, our order of subterranean
government

our national anthem... bluegrass... culture hinged on musical
       interpretations of the greenery
we're in the worm world now, we exchange our services for soil,
       we try words & get leachate instead
the long futch[23] of our bodies adding (motley) fluids to the discourse

rattling on about who we used to be, nocturnal activity,
       affected by the light
asking you ... babe what's wrong ... you've barely touched
       your faecal matter

---

23. Futch, gay slang meaning Femme/Butch. To have both masculine and feminine qualities. To be between or to elude categories.

in the real world a year has squirmed by between us

what if all this time passes and we become unrecognisable?

i've regressed back into the closet... poked in the ass

repeatedly by corporate brogues until i give up &

surrender... investing in stocks

i'll have to forget you to preserve my sense of self !!

i'll have to forget you rather than

accept the terms for your departure !! i'd be holed up in my attic

irreversibly wronged

& left with no choice but to become Lady Havisham... rock

sadistically through each day

speaking to no-one... instead of respecting the ever-elusive

passage of time

those school days... long gone... our sexuality smacked open like

a (hairy) coconut at the fair

when spring did to us what viagra does for blood... when blood

did to us what spring does to worms... i would slip grass

into your mouth   ask you to trust me   hahaha!

i am bringing up betrayals to diminish this new one

i am releasing my jealousy into the wind... but it

persists like parmelia... taking from trees...

conjures you talking amongst yourselves, *measuring*

   moments by how many worms ago they occurred
& the more the worms the less the reason

   you have to keep me in your illustrious roster

despite your loss of faith i'm still right here

   still wanting to marvel at a small thrush in flight
still yearning to commit public indecency

   (with you) & appreciate the most creative technique;
raise up a whole wardrobes worth of worms knowing

   it all comes down to this

CALAMITY!

pinyon pines;   salted greasewood,

mainly a displaced tooth. verb.) to calamity jane
where i came from, to put my feelings in a long toed boot
and kick up the dust of this small town. always mistaken for
a cactus in a coarse layer of sand / bringing harm to anyone
who tries to touch me, to leave 'em guessing what exactly i am,
who i really want to fuck. the source of that bright pink spark
in my eye; an ancient astral fire, the rabbit warren where birth
is just another cartoon donut torn wide and where next to look then?
when neither cosmic nor animal in the desert provide? why, wild bill's

belt buckle! i left my desire in deadwood, going crazy with the saloon flies. better than sex (in most ways). my wagon, my loot,
an entire ghost town abandoned in my honour. to have a home for dysfunction. to have my wildness find a permanent place to rest,
i'd give up glory for good. first i was a woman wishing she was a lizard splayed on some californian rock. next i was sunlight on
stone; the genderless breeze, hushing the lizard's green back. amorphously a mother
wherever i go. now shooting bullets into a sugeuro for practise, janeing up saliva,
a mix of tobacco and moonshine, trousers janed down and janeing
my name in piss for the stars.

48

CAPER IN THE CASTRO[24]

Before Castro 'we weren't just in closets we were under rocks'
— D.Jones

if you ever woke up in a bar slinging the word "sheesh" around like a vocal lasso; ever lost a bet to a hard boiled detective with a drinking problem, thought about throwing a lit zippo into the trash under the barely perceptible gutter; ever longed to be unembarrassed in public, appreciating the digital masonry, waxing lyrical about the hypercard brick, the expressionist ivy; if you ever redesigned yourself on m.s paint, transported by the black diamonds in their shading, the earnest fire escapes leading up to their roofs; ever spent large pockets of time humanizing the interface, like florence nightingale in the hospital tents of your desktop; ever grew so tired of being careful not to antagonise the script, gathered useless items in your inventory; if you ever wrote inside a notebook where the pages go on and on; ever imagined a background of unaffordable synth, relied heavily on silence to tell the story you could not; i'm a foley artist telling you i love you using non-human sounds.

---

24. 'Caper in the Castro' was the world's first LGBTQ+ video game developed by C.M Ralph and released in 1989.

HAYAO MIYAZAKI DIRECTS MY BIOPIC[25]

and leaves

melodrama

in a trunk

under his bed

in this film i

was once a

girl but i

became a

bear when i

ate the boy

ten seconds in

he wouldn't

stop going on

about saving me

miyazaki's rhipsalis

is epiphytic

is consistent is

a kind parasite

and it grows

from each one of

25. Miyazaki was once recorded, during an interview, saying he doesn't write about romantic love, instead about "two characters who mutually inspire each other to live."

my cotton wool

ears the last time i

heard language it

broke my heart

in five places

i spent the

winter knocked out

under rocks while

they were busy

licking lichen from

birds everything here

is lime green

and sour i

fish and spit

badly i get

salt in my eyes

a bear with

cher bono's voice

shivers every morning

look at the treacherous

mountains aren't

they sublime

here i've lived

so long i've

become a myth

in reality this

film is five small

minutes and like

most things

when they end

you don't know

whether to

laugh

or cry

ACKNOWLEDGEMENTS

This book has been made possible thanks to the loving support of friends, poets and family who believed in me even when I had nothing to show for it. That in itself, has been the most powerful kind of magic.

Thank you to Stephen, Em and Grace. Our pub meets, poem swaps and friendship have been like jet fuel for the writing of this pamphlet. Thank you Nathan Filer, for your wise words, humour and enthusiasm from BSU and beyond. I'm so very glad we met. Thank you Tim Liardet — I have negotiated with your ghost while writing these poems. Thank you to my Bath Spa coursemates — you became my chosen family when I needed one the most. To Fin, to Gem, to Sofia and our silly symbiosis; let's start that commune. To Kit and Aden, even though you forgot to invite me to worm charming(!)

Thank you to the editors at *Bi+Lines* (Helen Bowell) and *fourteen poems* (Ben Townley-Canning), *BathInk,* and The Plaza Prizes for publishing previous versions of the poems in this pamphlet. Thank you to the facilitators of the Poetry Society's Young Critics Scheme; Helen Bowell (again!) and Cia Mangat. Ella Frears, thank you for your wisdom and mentorship when these poems were "flinging thoughts like a mad thing." Thank you to Aaron Kent at Broken Sleep Books for his hard work, time and patience when putting together this collection with me.

Thank you to Elizabeth for your bright pink rabbits and gentle reminders that I don't have to do everything on my own. Your love has flown here like a gargoyle from the 13th century!

Kinder Parasites was written considering a kind of queer mutuality. What it means to feed and be fed from and how we honour ourselves and a community. With this in mind, Kinder Parasites is for the butches, the femmes, the fruits, the dykes, the gender benders, the drag queens and kings, the forerunners of our freedom. The fight is never over.

For whatever mothers you. What dares to daughter you.

LAY OUT YOUR UNREST